Dog
TRIVIA

Published by Willow Creek Press, Inc.
P.O. Box 147, Minocqua, Wisconsin 54548

Printed in the United States

Dog
TRIVIA

OVER 200 PAWESOME CANINE
FACTS FOR DOG LOVERS

🗗 WILLOW CREEK PRESS®

RIN TIN TIN WAS A RESCUE DOG.
FOUND BY A U.S. SERVICEMAN
AS AN ABANDONED PUPPY ON
A WWI EUROPEAN BATTLEFIELD,
"RINTY" EVENTUALLY HEADED TO
HOLLYWOOD TO STAR IN 27 FILMS.

DOGS ON AVERAGE HAVE 50 SPINAL VERTEBRAE.
HUMANS HAVE ONLY 33.

THE AMERICAN KENNEL CLUB
RECOGNIZES ONLY 189 BREEDS.

THE BLOODHOUND'S FLOPPY EARS FAN
GROUND SCENT INTO THE AIR AND THEIR
NOSE WHEN ACTIVELY TRACKING.

PUPPY TEETH FALL OUT AFTER
ABOUT SIX TO SEVEN WEEKS.

MORE THAN HALF OF ALL U.S.
PRESIDENTS HAVE OWNED DOGS.

45% OF DOGS SLEEP IN
THEIR OWNER'S BEDS.

TODAY'S DOG EVOLVED FROM
MIACIS - A CREATURE THAT
LIVED 50 MILLION YEARS AGO.

THE IRISH WOLFHOUND IS THE TALLEST DOG BREED. MALES CAN REACH 35" TALL.

AVOCADOS, GARLIC, ONIONS, AND GRAPES ARE FOODS THAT CAN BE TOXIC TO DOGS.

MONKS DEVELOPED THE ST. BERNARD BREED IN THE 17TH CENTURY. OVER THE YEARS THESE BRAVE DOGS HAVE BEEN RESPONSIBLE FOR THOUSANDS OF MOUNTAIN RESCUES.

THE MOVIE CHARACTER "LASSIE" WAS BILLED AS A FEMALE ROUGH COLLIE WHEN IN FACT EVERY DOG TO PLAY THE ROLE WAS MALE.

THE PAPILLON DERIVED ITS NAME FROM THE FRENCH WORD FOR BUTTERFLY. THE BREED'S WINGLIKE EARS INSPIRED THE APPELLATION.

DOGS ARE CONTENT OR RELAXED WHEN THEIR TAIL IS LEVEL WITH THEIR BODY. DOGS HOLDING THEIR TAIL LOW INDICATES A SIGN OF INSECURITY.

THE LOOSE FRENCH
TRANSLATION FOR THE BASSET
HOUND IS "RATHER LOW."

LABRADOR RETRIEVERS,
GOLDEN RETRIEVERS,
CHESAPEAKE BAY RETRIEVERS,
AND NEWFOUNDLANDS
ALL HAVE WEBBED FEET.
NOT COINCIDENTALLY,
ALL FOUR BREEDS ARE
REMARKABLE SWIMMERS.

A DOG FOCUSES ON SPECIFIC SOUNDS
BY CLOSING OFF PARTS OF ITS EARS.

PUPPIES ARE BORN WITH THEIR
EARS AND EYES SHUT. THEY OPEN
WITHIN TWO WEEKS OF BIRTH.

THE FIRST CLONED DOG WAS AN
AFGHAN HOUND NAMED "SNUPPY."

THE STANDARD POODLE WAS BRED
TO RETRIEVE WATERFOWL.

DACHSHUND IS GERMAN
FOR "BADGER DOG."

THOUGH IT'S NOT FULLY
UNDERSTOOD WHY, SHAR-PEI
AND CHOW CHOW ARE THE
ONLY TWO DOG BREEDS
WITH FULLY BLACK TONGUES.

"DAVY" THE WHIPPET IS IN THE RECORD BOOK FOR "THE LONGEST FLYING DISC THROW CAUGHT BY A DOG."

BECAUSE NEUTERING AND SPAYING REDUCE
CANCER RISKS, DOGS THAT ARE "FIXED" TEND
TO LIVE LONGER THAN DOGS THAT ARE NOT.

"BINGO" IS THE NAME OF THE DOG
ON THE CRACKER JACK BOX.

THE BOSTON TERRIER WAS THE FIRST
AMERICAN DOG BREED TO BE RECOGNIZED
BY THE AMERICAN KENNEL CLUB.

LAPLANDERS USE FINNISH LAPPHUNDS TO HUNT PUFFINS. THE NORWEGIAN LUNDEHUND WAS ALSO BRED FOR THE SAME PURPOSE.

STUDIES INDICATE THAT DOGS RECOGNIZE HUMAN FACIAL EMOTIONS.

A DOG HAS BEEN DEEMED, "THE ONLY THING ON EARTH THAT LOVES YOU MORE THAN YOU LOVE THEMSELVES."

THE BOSTON TERRIER IS
THE OFFICIAL STATE DOG
OF MASSACHUSETTS.

THE AKC RECOGNIZES "SNOOPY" AS THE TOP DOG IN AMERICAN CULTURE.

BOXERS RECEIVED THEIR NAME DUE TO THEIR HABIT OF USING THEIR FRONT PAWS WHEN FIGHTING.

THE 1959 FILM, "THE SHAGGY DOG," STARRED SAM, AN OLD ENGLISH SHEEPDOG, WHOSE PAW PRINTS ARE STILL PRESERVED IN CEMENT AT THE BURBANK, CA ANIMAL SHELTER.

THE BULLMASTIFF WAS BRED TO CATCH CRIMINALS WITHOUT HURTING THEM.

BASENJIS CAN'T BARK, THEY YODEL.

DOGS RECOGNIZE UP TO 250
WORDS AND GESTURES.

BRIARDS WERE FIRST BROUGHT
FROM FRANCE TO TODAY'S U.S. IN
1789 BY THOMAS JEFFERSON.

THE AMERICAN ESKIMO DOG BREED
ORIGINATED IN GERMANY. THE BREED
WAS A POPULAR CIRCUS DOG.

TURNS OUT THAT SPUDS
MACKENZIE, THE BULL TERRIER
WHO REPRESENTED BUD
LIGHT BEER IN THE 1980S,
WAS IN FACT A FEMALE.

THE BEDLINGTON TERRIER IS NAMED
FOR THE TOWN OF BEDLINGTON
IN NORTHERN ENGLAND.

VIBRISSAE IS THE SCIENTIFIC
TERM FOR DOG WHISKERS.

BOY SCOUTS AND GIRL SCOUTS EARN
MERIT BADGES FOR DOG CARE.

BLOODHOUND TRACKING RESULTS CAN LEGALLY BE USED AS EVIDENCE IN COURT.

PRESIDENT LYNDON JOHNSON
HAD TWO BEAGLES NAMED
"HIM" AND "HER."

A DOG'S SENSE OF SMELL IS 100,000
TIMES STRONGER THAN OURS.

THE OLDEST KNOWN DOG BREED IS THE
SALUKI. THEY APPEAR IN EGYPTIAN
TOMBS GOING BACK TO 2,100 BC.

THE ENGLISH BULLDOG IS KNOWN
FOR ITS FLATULENCE.

DOGS ONLY HAVE SWEAT GLANDS
BETWEEN THEIR PAW PADS.

ACCORDING TO FOLKLORE, THE PERUVIAN INCA ORCHID RELIEVES ASTHMA AND STOMACH ACHES IN HUMANS BY "HUGGING" THEM.

DOGS INSTINCTIVELY EAT GRASS TO CLEANSE THEIR DIGESTIVE SYSTEM.

A CAIRN TERRIER NAMED "TERRY" PLAYED THE ROLE OF TOTO IN THE WIZARD OF OZ. TERRY LANDED HIS FIRST ROLE CO-STARRING WITH SHIRLEY TEMPLE IN THE MOVIE, BRIGHT EYES.

THE GREAT DANE IS THE STATE
DOG OF PENNSYLVANIA.

WITH THE AID OF A GERMAN SHEPHERD NAMED ORIENT, BILL IRWIN BECAME THE FIRST BLIND HIKER TO TRAVERSE THE 2,000-MILE APPALACHIAN TRAIL.

RUEFULLY CONSIDERED DOGS OF
THE UPPER CLASS, FRENCH MASTIFFS
WERE BROUGHT TO NEAR EXTINCTION
DURING THE FRENCH REVOLUTION.

ANCIENT CHINESE PEKINGESE
OWNERS CARRIED THE DOGS WITHIN
THE SLEEVES OF THEIR ROBES.

THE JAPANESE SPITZ IS CONSIDERED THE
NAUGHTIEST DOG BREED, FOLLOWED BY
MUDI, SCHICHON, AND COCKAPOO.

DAVY CROCKETT HAD A DOG NAMED "SPORT."
FORTUNATELY, HE DID NOT ACCOMPANY
DAVY TO THE ALAMO.

DOGS LICKING OTHER DOGS OR HUMANS
INDICATES A SIGN OF SUBMISSION.

ACCORDING TO THE AMERICAN HEART
ASSOCIATION, "INTERACTING WITH DOGS
CAN BOOST YOUR PRODUCTION OF 'HAPPY
HORMONES' SUCH AS OXYTOCIN, SEROTONIN,
AND DOPAMINE." THUS, DOG OWNERS TEND
TO LIVE LONGER THAN THOSE WITHOUT THEM.

DOGS ARE NOT COLOR BLIND
AS MANY BELIEVE. THEY SEE
IN YELLOW AND BLUE.

DOG FEET SMELL LIKE TORTILLAS OR CORN CHIPS. HARMLESS MICROORGANISMS ON THEIR PAW PADS AND BETWEEN THEIR TOES EMIT THE SCENT.

THE PRESENCE OF A DOG CAN LOWER YOUR BLOOD PRESSURE.

LESS THAN 20% OF LOST DOGS ARE EVER FOUND BECAUSE THE MAJORITY OF THOSE LACK ANY IDENTIFICATION.

CHIHUAHUAS ARE NAMED AFTER A STATE IN MEXICO.

DOGS CAN BE LEFT-PAWED
OR RIGHT-PAWED. SOME
DOGS ARE AMBILATERAL.

THE BICHON FRISE NAME TRANSLATES
TO "CURLY LAP DOG."

Q. WHAT HAPPENED WHEN THE DOG
ATTENDED THE FLEA CIRCUS?

A. HE STOLE THE SHOW.

DOGS USE THEIR TAILS, SHOULDERS, EYES, AND
EYEBROWS TO COMMUNICATE WITH HUMANS.

WIRE FOX TERRIERS HAVE 12 BEST IN
SHOW AWARDS FROM THE WESTMINSTER
DOG SHOW - THE MOST OF ANY BREED.

PUPPIES SLEEP 90% OF
THEIR FIRST 20 DAYS.

DALMATIAN PUPPIES ARE
BORN WITHOUT SPOTS.

"CERBERUS" WAS THE THREE-HEADED DOG
FROM GREEK MYTHOLOGY WHO GUARDED
THE GATES OF THE UNDERWORLD.

THE PERUVIAN INCA ORCHID IS
HAIRLESS EXCEPT FOR A MOHAWK
STYLE TUFT BETWEEN ITS EARS.

THE NORWEGIAN LUNDEHUND HAS SIX TOES
ON EACH FOOT. OTHER DOGS HAVE ONLY FOUR.

ADULT DOGS ARE
CONSIDERED AS SMART AS
A TWO-YEAR-OLD HUMAN.

DOGS SNIFF EACH OTHER'S BUTTS AS
A MEANS OF FRIENDLY INQUIRY.

TWO U.S. CUSTOMS DOGS, ROCKY AND BARKO, WERE SO SKILLED AT THEIR JOBS THAT MEXICAN DRUG LORDS PLACED A $300,000 BOUNTY ON THEM.

A RECENT STUDY SHOWED
DOGS BECOME JEALOUS
WHEN THEIR OWNERS
DISPLAY AFFECTION
TOWARDS OTHER ANIMALS.

DOGS DREAM - ESPECIALLY OLDER DOGS.

A DOG'S URINE CONTAINS DISTINCTIVE
SCENT MARKERS THAT COMMUNICATE
TO OTHER DOGS ITS PROXIMITY, SOCIAL
STANDING, SEX, AND AVAILABILITY.

FOURTH OF JULY AND ITS ASSOCIATED
FIREWORKS IS THE BUSIEST PERIOD FOR
ANIMAL SHELTERS TO ADMIT LOST DOGS.

DOGS CAN SMELL FEAR.

DOGS CURL UP IN A BALL WHEN SLEEPING TO PROTECT THEIR ORGANS FROM ATTACK.

FRENCH BULL DOGS ARE
NICKNAMED "FRENCHIES."

MARY, QUEEN OF SCOTS, IS ALLEGED TO
HAVE HAD HER ENGLISH TOY SPANIEL
WITH HER DURING HER BEHEADING.

WHILE IT SOMETIMES APPEARS SO,
DOGS DO NOT FEEL GUILT.

A DOG WILL SHAKE ITS HEAD WHEN
RELIEVED FROM A PERIOD OF TENSION.

THE LABRADOR RETRIEVER
WAS ONCE KNOWN AS ST.
JOHN'S NEWFOUNDLAND.

THE LYRICS TO THE BEATLES SONG, MARTHA MY DEAR, PAY TRIBUTE TO A DOG. "MARTHA" WAS THE NAME OF PAUL MCCARTNEY'S SHEEPDOG WHO HE DESCRIBED AS "A DEAR PET OF MINE."

TO FURTHER PERSONALIZE THE RECORDING, MCCARTNEY'S IS THE ONLY VOICE ON THE TRACK.

A GRAND BLEU DE GASCOGNE WAS GIFTED TO DOG-LOVER GEORGE WASHINGTON BY MARQUIS DE LAFAYETTE DURING THE AMERICAN REVOLUTIONARY WAR.

THE BIBLE MENTIONS DOGS 14 TIMES.

THE CHESAPEAKE BAY
RETRIEVER IS DESCENDED
FROM TWO PUPPIES
DISCOVERED ON AN
1807 SHIPWRECK.

ONLY NOBLES COULD OWN
GREYHOUNDS IN THE 11TH CENTURY.

DOGS HAVE THREE EYELIDS.
ONE IS THE NICTITATING MEMBRANE
WHICH IS USED TO KEEP THE EYES
LUBRICATED AND PROTECTED.

THE NATIONAL DOG OF FINLAND
IS THE FINNISH SPITZ.

THE COTON DE TULEAR IS THE
OFFICIAL DOG OF MADAGASCAR.
SADLY, THE EXTREMELY RARE BREED
IS CLOSE TO EXTINCTION.

JAPAN IN THE 1930S DEEMED THE
AINU, AKITA, AND KAI INU DOG
BREEDS "NATIONAL TREASURES."

NICK CARTER, A KENTUCKY
BLOODHOUND, IS SAID TO HAVE TRACKED
MORE THAN 600 CRIMINALS.

GEORGE WASHINGTON OWNED 30
FOXHOUNDS INCLUDING PERHAPS A
FAVORITE NAMED "SWEET LIPS."

THE AMERICAN COCKER
SPANIEL AND THE ENGLISH
COCKER SPANIEL WERE
OFFICIALLY CONSIDERED THE
SAME BREED UNTIL 1936.

30% OF DALMATIONS ARE DEAF IN ONE EAR. 5% ARE DEAF IN BOTH EARS.

ACCORDING TO THE GUINNESS WORLD
RECORDS, THE AFRICAN HUNTING DOG
IS THE MOST SUCCESSFUL LAND HUNTER
IN THE WORLD. 50% - 70% OF THEIR
INITIATED HUNTS PROVE SUCCESSFUL.

A DOG TILTS ITS HEAD WHEN CURIOUS
OR AWAITING NEW INFORMATION.

THE BEATLES PURPOSELY ADDED A
FREQUENCY THAT ONLY DOGS CAN HEAR
IN THE SONG, "A DAY IN THE LIFE."

RESEARCHERS BELIEVE THAT DOGS CAN
DETECT EARTH'S MAGNETIC FIELD.

A ONE-YEAR-OLD DOG IS AS PHYSICALLY
MATURE AS A 15-YEAR-OLD HUMAN.

THE MEXICAN HAIRLESS DOG WAS THOUGHT
SACRED BY THE AZTECS AND MAYA.

THE SCIENTIFIC NAME FOR
DOG IS CANIS FAMILIARIS.

THE SCOTTISH TERRIER IS A
GAME PIECE IN MONOPOLY.

THE AUSTRALIAN SHEPHERD DOG BREED
WAS ACTUALLY DEVELOPED IN THE U.S.

THE ALASKAN MALAMUTE IS ALASKA'S OFFICIAL STATE DOG.

CHINESE CRESTED DOGS
WERE USED AS SHIPBOARD
RAT CATCHERS.

42% OF U.S. HOUSEHOLDS HAVE
AT LEAST ONE DOG.

THE CHESAPEAKE BAY RETRIEVER IS THE
OFFICIAL STATE DOG OF MARYLAND.

HOVAWART IS DERIVED FROM THE
GERMAN TERM, "NIGHT WATCHMAN."

ON AVERAGE, MUTTS LIVE LONGER
THAN PUREBRED DOGS.

DOGS HAVE 78 CHROMOSOMES.
HUMANS HAVE ONLY 46.

THE CATAHOULA LEOPARD
DOG CLIMBS TREES.

A GROUP OF PUGS IS
CALLED A "GRUMBLE."

THE OLDEST DOG KNOWN
WAS BLUEY, AN AUSTRALIAN
CATTLE DOG WHO LIVED TO
THE AGE OF TWENTY-NINE.

KUVASZ TRANSLATES FROM TURKISH TO "ARMED GUARD OF NOBILITY."

THE GOLDEN RETRIEVER ORIGINALLY
CAME FROM SCOTLAND.

DOGS DON'T SWEAT LIKE
HUMANS BUT PANT TO
EMIT BODY HEAT.

RIN TIN TIN SIGNED ALL 22 OF HIS MOVIE CONTRACTS WITH HIS PAW PRINT. 🐾

FEMALE DOGS COME "INTO HEAT" FOR ABOUT 20 DAYS TWICE ANNUALLY.

MASTIFFS WORE ARMOR DURING ROMAN TIMES TO FIGHT KNIGHTS ON HORSEBACK.

BASSET HOUNDS CANNOT SWIM.

THE NEW GUINEA SINGING DOG IS A DISTINCT BREED WITH AN UNPREDICTABLE TENDENCY TO ROAM AND HUNT INDEPENDENT OF HUMANS.

IT IS ALSO ONE OF THE RAREST BREEDS IN THE WORLD.

DOGS YAWN DUE TO ANXIETY OR WEARINESS. THEY ALSO YAWN IN EMPATHY FOR HUMANS, PARTICULARLY THEIR OWNERS.

BASENJIS ARE KNOWN FOR THEIR CAT-LIKE PERSONALITY AND INDIFFERENCE TO TRAINING.

ROUGHLY 1 MILLION U.S. DOGS
HAVE BEEN NAMED AS PRIMARY
BENEFICIARIES IN THEIR
OWNER'S WILL.

A DOG'S EAR HAS OVER ONE DOZEN
MUSCLES. HUMANS HAVE JUST SIX.

GEORGE WASHINGTON HAD A DALMATIAN
HE NAMED "MADAME MOOSE."

DOGS CAN RECOGNIZE THEIR OWNERS
ON A TELEVISION SCREEN.

THE STANDARD POODLE'S NAME DERIVES
FROM THE GERMAN WORD, "PUDEL,"
MEANING "TO SPLASH IN WATER."

**THE SAINT BERNARD IS THE
HEAVIEST BREED IN THE WORLD.**

IT'S ESTIMATED THAT THE WORLD'S DOG
POPULATION EXCEEDS 900 MILLION.

THE FIRST TWO TIBETAN MASTIFFS
ARRIVED IN THE U.S. AS GIFTS TO
PRESIDENT DWIGHT EISENHOWER.

LOOKS MATTER: BOTH THE PEKINGESE
AND LOWCHEN ARE KNOWN AS
"LITTLE LION DOGS."

POINSETTIA, ALOE, AND BEGONIA
PLANTS ARE POISONOUS TO DOGS.

THE LARGEST RECORDED LITTER OF
PUPPIES (24) WAS BORN TO A MASTIFF.

DOGS HAVE TERRIFIC PERIPHERAL VISION
BECAUSE OF THEIR WIDE-SET EYES.

THERE ARE 703 BREEDS
OF PUREBRED DOG.

BORDER COLLIES, POODLES,
AND GERMAN SHEPHERDS
ARE THOUGHT TO BE THE MOST
INTELLIGENT OF BREEDS.

58% OF OWNERS INCLUDE THEIR DOGS
IN HOLIDAY AND FAMILY PORTRAITS.

A WET NOSE AIDS IN
KEEPING A DOG COOL DURING
HOT DAYS. IT ALSO HELPS IN
DECIPHERING SCENTS.

NEWFOUNDLANDS HAVE A NATURAL INSTINCT TO RESCUE PEOPLE FROM DANGER.

DOGS HAVE 1,700 TASTE BUDS COMPARED TO HUMANS 9,000.

THERE ARE EIGHT DESIGNATED CATEGORIES OF DOG BREEDS: TERRIERS, HOUNDS, SPORTING DOGS, NON-SPORTING DOGS, WORKING DOGS, HERDING DOGS, TOY DOGS, AND MISCELLANEOUS BREEDS.

CHIHUAHUA PUPPIES ARE BORN
WITH A "SOFT SPOT" IN THEIR
SKULLS - JUST LIKE HUMAN BABIES.
ALSO LIKE HUMAN BABIES, THE SOFT
SPOT DISAPPEARS OVER TIME.

THE LONGER A DOG'S NOSE
THE BETTER THEIR INTERNAL
COOLING SYSTEM OPERATES.

Q. WHY ARE DOGS TERRIBLE DANCERS?

A. THEY HAVE TWO LEFT FEET.

A PUPPY'S VISION IS NOT FULLY
DEVELOPED UNTIL AFTER A MONTH.

DOGS SENSE FREQUENCIES OF 30,000
TIMES PER SECOND. HUMANS DETECT
THEM AT 20,000 TIMES PER SECOND.

SPIKED COLLARS WERE
ORIGINALLY MADE TO PROTECT
DOGS FROM WOLF ATTACKS.

THE FOXHOUND IS THE OFFICIAL
STATE DOG OF VIRGINIA.

QUEEN ELIZABETH II WAS ONE OF THE
LONGEST-ESTABLISHED BREEDERS OF
PEMBROKE CORGIS IN THE WORLD.
SHE ALSO BRED A SPECIAL LINE
OF LABRADOR RETRIEVERS.

ALTHOUGH CONSIDERED OMNIVORES,
DOG DIETS ARE MAINLY MEAT-BASED.

DOG FOSSILS DATE BACK
TO 10,000 BC.

IN NYC'S CENTRAL PARK STANDS
THE STATUE OF "BALTO," A SIBERIAN
HUSKY SLED DOG WHO HELPED
DELIVER LIFESAVING DIPHTHERIA
TREATMENT TO NOME, AL IN 1925.

THE RHODESIAN RIDGEBACK WAS
BRED TO HUNT LIONS.

UNTIL 1964, THE NORFOLK TERRIER
AND THE NORWICH TERRIER WERE
CONSIDERED THE SAME BREED.

HAN DYNASTY STATUES CLOSELY
RESEMBLING THE CHINESE SHARPEI
DATE BACK 2,000 YEARS.

THE GIANT SCHNAUZER WAS EMPLOYED
TO GUARD GERMAN BREWERIES.

THE CHINOOK IS THE OFFICIAL
STATE DOG OF NEW HAMPSHIRE.

PUPPIES CAN BEGIN EATING REAL FOOD
ABOUT FOUR WEEKS AFTER BIRTH.

THREE DOGS WERE RESCUED BEFORE THE
SINKING OF THE TITANIC. TWO POMERANIANS
AND A PEKINGESE WERE SMALL BREEDS THAT
COULD BE ACCOMMODATED ON LIFEBOATS.

THE BLACK AND TAN COONHOUND IS
ALLEGEDLY KNOWN FOR STEALING FOOD.

DOGS DON'T CHEW FOOD BUT
SWALLOW IT IN CHUNKS.

A PERSON WHO HUNTS
WITH A BEAGLE IS KNOWN
AS A "BEAGLER."

GREATER SWISS MOUNTAIN DOGS WERE BRED TO PULL CARTS. THE INTRODUCTION OF THE AUTOMOBILE NEGATIVELY IMPACTED THE BREED'S POPULARITY.

BREED DEPENDENT, A NORMAL DOG'S HEARTBEAT IS BETWEEN 60 AND 140 BEATS PER MINUTE.

HUMANS HAVE BETTER DEPTH PERCEPTION THAN DOGS, BUT DOGS HAVE BETTER LOW-LIGHT VISION THAN US.

IT'S IMPORTANT FOR A DOG'S
PHYSICAL HEALTH TO EXERCISE
FREQUENTLY. PHYSICAL ACTIVITY ALSO
PLAYS A LARGE ROLE IN ITS MENTAL
HEALTH AND POSITIVE BEHAVIOR.

THE U.S. HAS MORE PET DOGS THAN ANY OTHER NATION IN THE WORLD. FRANCE HAS THE WORLD'S SECOND LARGEST PET DOG POPULATION.

THE HAVANESE IS THE
NATIONAL DOG OF CUBA.

AT LAST REPORT, ONLY 350 CESKY
TERRIERS EXIST IN THE WORLD.

ALEXANDER THE GREAT NAMED A CITY
AFTER HIS FAVORITE DOG, "PERITAS."
PERITAS DEFENDED ALEXANDER
FROM AN ATTACKING ELEPHANT.

DOGS CAN BE TRAINED TO SENSE AND
DETECT EPILEPTIC SEIZURES IN HUMANS.

TEDDY ROOSEVELT'S DOG, PETE, RIPPED
THE PANTS OFF A FRENCH AMBASSADOR
WHO WAS VISITING THE WHITE HOUSE.

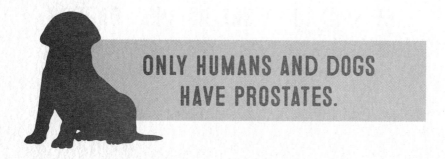

ONLY HUMANS AND DOGS
HAVE PROSTATES.

TO BEST ACCUSTOM DOGS TO HUMANS
THEY SHOULD MAKE CONTACT WITH US
NO LATER THAN FOUR WEEKS OLD.

A DOG'S BODY TEMPERATURE RANGES FROM
101 TO 102.5 DEGREES FAHRENHEIT.

NEWFOUNDLANDS AND GREAT DANES ARE
CONSIDERED THE QUIETEST DOG BREEDS.
ON THE OTHER HAND, BEAGLES AND HUSKIES
ARE SAID TO BE THE NOISIEST BREEDS.

THE LABRADOR RETRIEVER IS
THE MOST POPULAR BREED
IN THE U.S. (FOLLOWED BY
THE GERMAN SHEPHERD
AND GOLDEN RETRIEVER)

THE ICELAND SHEEPDOG IS
THOUGHT TO ORIGINATE FROM
VIKING BREEDERS.

A DOG'S SKELETON IS COMPOSED
OF 319 BONES. HUMANS HAVE AN
AVERAGE OF 206 TO 213.

AN ENGLISH MASTIFF NAMED "ZORBA"
WEIGHED 343 POUNDS. HE'S THE
HEAVIEST DOG EVER RECORDED.

A DOG'S MOUTH APPLIES 150-200 POUNDS
OF PRESSURE PER SQUARE INCH. SOME
DOGS ARE EVEN ON RECORD EXERTING
450 POUNDS PER SQUARE INCH.

IN THE U.S., OBESITY IS THE NUMBER
ONE HEALTH PROBLEM FOR DOGS.

RAPID TAIL-WAGGING DOES NOT NECESSARILY
MEAN A DOG IS HAPPY. BUT IT DOES
MEANS IT'S EXCITED ABOUT SOMETHING.

ONE STUDY SHOWS THAT 87% OF U.S. DOG
OWNERS REPORT THEIR DOGS LIE BESIDE
THEM OR AT THEIR FEET WHILE WATCHING TV.

TERRIER BREEDS WERE BRED TO
CONTROL RODENT POPULATIONS.

DOGS MAY BE SEPARATE BY BREED,
BUT THEY ARE ALL THE SAME SPECIES.

"GIDGET" IS THE NAME OF
THE TACO BELL DOG.
SHE BECAME FAMOUS FOR SAYING
"YO QUIERO TACO BELL" DURING
TELEVISION COMMERCIALS.

ENGLISH SPRINGER SPANIELS WERE BRED
TO BE HUNTING DOGS. SPECIFICALLY, THEY
WERE USED TO "FLUSH" OR "SPRING" GAME,
MEANING THEY WOULD CHASE BIRDS INTO
FLIGHT SO THAT HUNTERS WOULD THEN SHOOT.

IN 1871, CHARLES DARWIN OBSERVED
THAT "DOGS SHOW WHAT MAY BE FAIRLY
CALLED A SENSE OF HUMOR, AS DISTINCT
FROM MERE PLAY." DOG VOCALIZATIONS
WHEN AT PLAY HAVE BEEN INTERPRETED
BY RESEARCHERS AS LAUGHTER.

DOG'S NOSE PRINTS ARE AS UNIQUE AS
HUMAN FINGERPRINTS. SOME COMPANIES
PLACE INDIVIDUAL NOSE PRINTS ON
RECORD TO AID IN FINDING LOST DOGS.

THE ANCIENT EGYPTIANS NOT ONLY WORSHIPED CATS BUT DOGS AS WELL.

A RECENT POLL REVEALS THAT 33% OF DOG OWNERS ADMIT TO - HAVING AT LEAST ONCE TALKED TO THEIR DOGS ON THE PHONE OR LEAVING VOICE MESSAGES.

BLOODHOUNDS CAN IDENTIFY
NUMEROUS SCENTS SIMULTANEOUSLY.

PREGNANT DOGS CARRY THEIR PUPPIES FOR ABOUT 60 DAYS PRIOR TO BIRTH.

CAVALIER KING CHARLES SPANIELS WERE COVETED BY THE ENGLISH MONARCHY AS FOOT WARMERS AS WELL AS LAP DOGS.

DOGS LICKING OTHER DOGS OR HUMANS INDICATES A SIGN OF SUBMISSION.

LIKE WOLVES, DOGS ARE NATURAL PACK ANIMALS.

DOGS INDICATE THEIR DESIRE TO PLAY BY LOWERING THEIR CHEST AND HEAD TO THE GROUND WITH THE REAR END AND TAIL UP. THIS BEHAVIOR IS KNOWN AS THE "PLAY BOW".

DOGS CAN SENSE TIME. THEY DEMONSTRATE THIS BY ANTICIPATING MEAL TIME AND PREDICTING WALK TIME.

IN 1957, THE RUSSIAN DOG LAIKA BECAME THE FIRST LIVING CREATURE IN SPACE. JFK'S TERRIER "CHARLIE" FATHERED FOUR PUPPIES WITH HER DAUGHTER.

WELSH FARMERS BRED AND USED
CORGIS AS CATTLE HERDERS.
THEIR LOW-SLUNG FRAME MADE IT
DIFFICULT FOR CATTLE TO KICK THEM.

RIN TIN TIN WAS NOMINATED BEST ACTOR AT THE 1929 ACADEMY AWARDS. HE LOST OUT TO MERE HUMAN EMIL JENNINGS.

SMALL DOGS DETECT HIGHER NOISE FREQUENCIES THAN LARGER DOGS. THEIR SENSITIVITY TO SOUND MAY EXPLAIN THEIR FRIGHTENED REACTIONS DURING THUNDERSTORMS.

70% OF OWNERS SIGN THEIR DOG'S NAME ON HOLIDAY CARDS.

WHISKERS HELP DOGS SEE AND NAVIGATE IN THE DARK.

DOGS DISLIKE BEING HUGGED.
BEING HELD RENDERS THEM
IMMOBILE AND EXERTS FEARFUL
DOMINANCE OVER THEM

GREYHOUNDS CAN REACH PEAK
SPEEDS OF OVER 40 MPH.